D1710026

SUPER CHIEFS!

CELEBRATING KANSAS CITY'S CHAMPIONSHIP SEASON

Book design by **Josh Crutchmer**

Photos courtesy of Getty Images and AP Images

© 2023 KCI Sports Publishing
All Rights reserved. Except for use in a review, the reproduction or utilization of this work in any form or by electronic, mechanical, or other means, now known or hereafter invented, including xerography, photocopying, and recording, and in any information storage and retrieval system, is forbidden without the written permission of the publisher.

ISBN: 978-1957005-16-4

Printed in the United States of America

Introduction	4
Super Bowl LVII | **Chiefs vs. Eagles**	8
Regular Season | **Chiefs 44, Cardinals 21**	22
Regular Season | **Chiefs 27, Chargers 24**	26
Regular Season | **Colts 20, Chiefs 17**	30
Regular Season | **Chiefs 41, Buccaneers 31**	32
Chiefs Feature | **Jerick McKinnon**	36
Regular Season | **Chiefs 30, Raiders 29**	38
Regular Season | **Bills 24, Chiefs 20**	42
Regular Season | **Chiefs 44, 49ers 23**	44
Regular Season | **Chiefs 20, Titans 17** (OT)	48
Chiefs Feature | **Frank Clark and Chris Jones**	54
Regular Season | **Chiefs 27, Jaguars 17**	58
Regular Season | **Chiefs 30, Chargers 27**	62
Regular Season | **Chiefs 26, Rams 10**	66
Regular Season | **Bengals 27, Chiefs 24**	70
Chiefs Feature | **Andy Reid**	72
Regular Season | **Chiefs 34, Broncos 28**	76
Regular Season | **Chiefs 30, Texans 24** (OT)	80
Regular Season | **Chiefs 24, Seahawks 10**	88
Regular Season | **Chiefs 27, Broncos 24**	92
Regular Season | **Chiefs 31, Raiders 13**	96
Chiefs Feature | **Jason Kelce**	100
Divisional Playoffs | **Chiefs 27, Jaguars 20**	102
Chiefs Feature | **Patrick Mahomes**	112
AFC Championship | **Chiefs 23, Bengals 20**	116

Masterpiece!

THE KANSAS CITY CHIEFS HAVE DONE IT AGAIN — WORLD CHAMPIONS!

Let the celebration and dynasty talk begin!

In a season where many predicted a step back offensively after trading away star receiver Tyreek Hill, Kansas City reloaded by signing Juju Smith-Schuster and Marquez Valdes-Scantling along with mid-season trade pickup Kadarius Toney that provided a stable of capable playmakers. The Chiefs were able to keep a laser-like focus on the task at hand winning an incredible nine games by seven or fewer points. Led by the unflappable Patrick Mahomes, the Chiefs responded in tight games with the clutch plays needed to come out on top.

That perseverance, teamwork and will to win that made up the DNA of this Chiefs team was on full display week after week.

In the following pages enjoy a trip down memory lane of this championship season that came to its jubilant conclusion with the Super Bowl LVII victory in Arizona over a very talented Philadelphia Eagles team.

Heartfelt congratulations go out to the Hunt family, GM Brett Veach, Coach Reid and his staff, and the entire team on their incredible accomplishments this season. Celebrate this season Kansas City fans, and save this book to revisit the Chiefs' magical moments and this unforgettable team - both stars and role players — who rewarded your faith with another NFL Championship.

Congratulations Chiefs Kingdom!

Patrick Mahomes holds the Lombardi Trophy as he is joined by teammates on the podium after Kansas City won Super Bowl LVII over the Eagles, 38-35.

Chiefs 38, Eagles 35 February 12, 2023

Magic in the Desert

Mahomes Rallies Chiefs from First-Half Deficit to Second Super Bowl Title

GLENDALE, Ariz. —

PATRICK MAHOMES SHOOK OFF AN ANKLE INJURY, TURNED BACK INTO A magician and pulled out another comeback on the biggest stage to help the Kansas City Chiefs win their second Super Bowl in four years.

Mahomes threw two touchdown passes in the fourth quarter and scrambled 26 yards on the go-ahead drive before Harrison Butker kicked a 27-yard field goal with 8 seconds left to give the Chiefs a 38-35 victory over the Philadelphia Eagles on Sunday night.

"He's the MVP," Chiefs coach Andy Reid said about Mahomes. "That's all that needs to be said. MVP. And you saw it tonight."

Mahomes and Jalen Hurts excelled in the first Super Bowl matchup featuring two Black starting QBs. But Mahomes, the two-time AP NFL MVP, turned it up in the second half after reaggravating a sprained right ankle. He earned his second Super Bowl MVP award, too.

"It took everybody to win the games. We're Super Bowl champs, baby," Mahomes shouted on stage as red and yellow confetti littered the field.

Reid, who couldn't win the big game in Philadelphia, beat his former team to earn his second ring with Mahomes and the Chiefs.

"We wanted to get this so bad for him," Travis Kelce said. "His legacy in Philly lives on forever. The organization loves him."

With the score tied at 35-35, the Eagles tried to let the Chiefs score a touchdown with under two minutes left so they could get the ball back after a defensive holding call on cornerback James Bradberry on third-and-8 gave Kansas City a first down. But Jerick McKinnon slid at the 2, forcing the Eagles to use their last timeout.

After Mahomes took a knee two times, Butker nailed his kick, sending thousands of red-clad Chiefs fans into a frenzy.

The Chiefs won their second Super Bowl following the 2019 season, 50 years after the first one. It took just three years to get another Lombardi.

Chiefs fans were outnumbered in the stadium, but they did their part to silence the boisterous Philly fans with the tomahawk chop chant.

Down 24-14 with a limping Mahomes, the Chiefs (17-3) followed up Rihanna's electrifying halftime performance with a sensational offensive outburst.

"Everybody had that determination, that look in their eye," Kelce said.

Mahomes, who suffered a high ankle sprain in the divisional round, hurt it again on a 3-yard scramble late in the second quarter. He limped off the field but showed no ill effects on Kansas City's next possession.

Mahomes slipped — several players lost their footing on the natural grass surface — in the pocket yet somehow regained his balance and scrambled 14 yards to the Eagles 4, setting up Isiah Pacheco's 1-yard TD run that cut the deficit to 24-21.

After Jake Elliott's 33-yard field goal extended Philadelphia's lead to 27-21, the Chiefs struck again.

Chiefs quarterback and Super Bowl MVP Patrick Mahomes holds the Lombardi Trophy after Kansas City won Super Bowl LVII.

Mahomes tossed a 5-yard TD pass to a wide-open Kadarius Toney to give Kansas City its first lead, 28-27, early in the fourth quarter.

The Chiefs tightened up their defense, forcing Philly to punt. Then Toney returned a line-drive kick 65 yards to the Eagles 5 for the longest punt return in Super Bowl history.

On third down from the 4, Mahomes connected with Skyy Moore to extend their lead to 35-27. Moore also was wide open on the play.

But the Eagles wouldn't go away.

Hurts hit DeVonta Smith for a 46-yard gain to the Chiefs and ran in for his third score of the game. He also ran in for the 2-point conversion to tie it at 35-35 with 5:15 to go.

As "Fly! Eagles! Fly!" reverberated throughout the stadium, Mahomes and the Chiefs went back to work.

The 27-year-old Mahomes became the third player to win his second NFL MVP award before age 28. He also became the youngest QB to start three Super Bowls. Then, Mahomes became the first player to win the Super Bowl the same season he was MVP after nine straight players lost.

Just five years after winning the first Super Bowl in franchise history, the Eagles (16-4) came close with a different coach and new quarterback. Nick Sirianni replaced Doug Pederson in 2021 and Hurts took over for Carson Wentz in late 2020.

Hurts set a Super Bowl record with 70 yards rushing and tied a record with three rushing scores. He also threw for 304 yards and one TD.

The Eagles marched 75 yards down

Chiefs receiver Kadarius Toney returns a punt 65 yards to set the Chiefs up to take a 35-27 lead in the fourth quarter of the Super Bowl.

the field with Hurts scoring from the 1 for a 7-0 lead, and controlled the ball for almost 22 minutes in the first half.

Hurts, who missed two games late in the season with a shoulder injury, had no trouble throwing a perfect deep ball to A.J. Brown, giving the Eagles a 14-7 lead with a 45-yard connection on the first play of the second quarter.

But Hurts then made a rare mistake on the next drive when he fumbled without being hit while scrambling away from pressure. Nick Bolton picked it up and raced 36 yards for a score that made it 14-14. Hurts had just eight turnovers this season, six picks and two fumbles.

Undeterred, Hurts kept running.

He took off for 14 yards on the first play after the fumble. On fourth-and-5 from Chiefs 44, Hurts ran 28 yards. He finished off the drive with a 4-yard TD run to put Philadelphia ahead 21-14.

Elliott kicked a 35-yard field goal to send the Eagles into halftime leading 24-14.

Mahomes finished 21 of 27 for 182 yards with three TDs and no turnovers. He ran for 44 yards.

Mahomes connected with Kelce on an 18-yard TD pass in the right corner to tie it at 7-7 in the first quarter. The Chiefs' All-Pro tight end and Eagles All-Pro center Jason Kelce became the first set of brothers to play against each other in the Super Bowl.

Eagles fans turned State Farm Stadium into a sea of green, chanting "E-A-G-L-E-S!" and singing the team's fight song after each score. But they left disappointed.

Kansas City kicker Harrison Butker watches the game-winning field goal against Philadelphia.

Patrick Mahomes eludes Eagles linebacker Haason Reddick as teammate Jerick McKinnon looks for an opening in the first half.

Chiefs receiver Skyy Moore celebrates scoring on a four-yard pass from Patrick Mahomes in the fourth quarter against the Eagles.

Travis Kelce hauls in the Chiefs' first score of the game in front of Eagles safety Marcus Epps in the first quarter.

Kansas City linebacker Nick Bolton runs to the end zone to score on a fumble recovery in the first half.

Chiefs 44, Cardinals 21 September 11, 2022

Opening Statement

Mahomes Starts off Red Hot as Chiefs Pound Cardinals to Start Season

GLENDALE, Ariz. —

KANSAS CITY COACH ANDY REID LOOKED SLIGHTLY PERPLEXED DURING Sunday's postgame press conference when asked why his quarterback Patrick Mahomes is so good in season openers.

Reid didn't notice any difference.

"He's pretty good all the time," he said with a slight grin. "We're lucky to have him."

Mahomes threw for 360 yards and five touchdowns, Clyde Edwards-Helaire caught two touchdown passes and the Chiefs rolled to an impressive 44-21 road win over the Arizona Cardinals in the opener for both teams.

The game was never in doubt after the opening minutes, with Mahomes picking apart the Cardinals' defense with his usual array of good decisions and deft passing touch. The quarterback was playing his first NFL game against Kliff Kingsbury, who coached Mahomes in college at Texas Tech and now leads the Cardinals.

The student put on quite a show for his mentor: The 2018 MVP threw three touchdown passes on Kansas City's first three drives.

After his fourth touchdown, he turned toward the Cardinals' sideline for a little trash talk, holding up four fingers to remind them of the damage he had already caused against the Arizona defense.

Mahomes said no matter how successful he becomes he'll always feel like the underdog. He's now 5-0 in season openers, throwing 18 touchdowns and zero interceptions.

"I'm just a guy from Texas Tech they said couldn't play in the NFL," Mahomes said. "I've always had that mindset of proving we're the Kansas City Chiefs, we still can win the AFC Championship, win the AFC West and win the Super Bowl."

Tight end Travis Kelce caught eight passes for 121 yards and a touchdown. It was his 30th career game with at least 100 yards receiving. Kansas City outgained Arizona 488 yards to 282. Mahomes completed 30 of 39 passes.

"We always believed we were going to go out there and put on a show," Mahomes said. "Guys did that."

The onslaught started in a hurry.

Kansas City jumped out to a 7-0 lead on the opening drive, capping an 11-play, 75-yard march with a 9-yard touchdown pass from Mahomes to Kelce. The Chiefs pushed ahead 14-0 later in the first on a nifty play from Mahomes, who threw an underhanded shovel pass to Edwards-Helaire for the 3-yard score.

The Chiefs led 23-7 by halftime after Harrison Butker, who missed part of the first half with a left ankle injury, made a 54-yard field goal with two seconds left in the second quarter.

Kansas City — which is trying to make the AFC title game for a fifth straight season — had a 37-7 advantage by the fourth quarter.

It was a rough start for Arizona, which also suffered through a brutal ending to 2021. The Cardinals have lost six of seven games dating to last season, including the playoffs.

Patrick Mahomes threw for 360 yards and five touchdowns in an opening-week victory over Arizona.

Chiefs running back Clyde Edwards-Helaire celebrates after a touchdown with wide receiver Mecole Hardman.

Chiefs 27, Chargers 24   September 15, 2022

Watson's Moment in the Sun

Unheralded Defender Seals Kansas City Rally With Critical Interception

KANSAS CITY, Mo. —

IN A SHOWDOWN BETWEEN THE CHIEFS AND CHARGERS, TWO OF THE league's best teams led by two of the game's bright young quarterbacks, an unheralded seventh-round draft pick who a few years ago was working alongside his mother in a Wendy's restaurant stole the show.

The Chiefs' Jaylen Watson picked off Justin Herbert at the goal line early in the fourth quarter Thursday night, headed the other way and was never touched on a 99-yard go-ahead touchdown that propelled Kansas City to a 27-24 victory.

"I don't even remember what happened at that moment," Watson said later. "It's all so surreal."

Chiefs quarterback Patrick Mahomes threw for 235 yards with TD passes to Jerick McKinnon and Justin Watson, and fill-in kicker Matt Ammendola was perfect in place of injured Harrison Butker. But it was the Chiefs' defense, and Watson's highlight-reel interception, that allowed Kansas City (2-0) to overcome its early problems in an early divisional test.

"The thing that I'm most proud of," Chiefs coach Andy Reid said, "is that we stuck together. Nobody pointed any fingers."

Two series after Watson's go-ahead touchdown, things got even worse for the Chargers (1-1) when Herbert was drilled by defensive end Mike Danna while delivering a throw. He left the field clutching his side, returned one play later, then threw an incompletion that forced the Chargers to punt while trailing 24-17.

Clyde Edwards-Helaire promptly split the defense on a 52-yard run to set up a field goal for Kansas City.

Herbert, who finished with 334 yards and three touchdown passes, gamely tried to keep the Chargers alive. He threw a 36-yard dart on fourth down to extend their ensuing possession, then hit Joshua Palmer in the back of the end zone on fourth-and-goal to pull Los Angeles within 27-24 with just over a minute to go.

Kansas City recovered the onside kick and ran out the clock to end the game.

"You're not going to see a quarterback in any level of football play tougher and do more for his team and will his team and give them a chance than him," Chargers coach Brandon Staley said of Herbert, who was getting X-rays and wasn't available after the game. "There's nobody who can do what he can do. Nobody. He showed a lot of guts.

"He showed what he shows us every day, that we're never out of the fight. He brought us back and gave us a chance."

The highly anticipated showdown between two of the league's most prolific quarterbacks, each surrounded by premier playmakers, turned out early on to be a defensive slugfest.

The Chargers held the Chiefs to 13 yards in the first quarter, thanks to relentless pressure from Joey Bosa and Khalil Mack and the fact that Derwin James Jr. was just about everywhere, and kept a team that scored 44 points last week in Arizona off the scoreboard until Mahomes slung a sidearm pass to McKinnon early in the second quarter.

Kansas City tight end Travis Kelce is upended by Chargers safety Derwin James Jr. as cornerback J.C. Jackson assists.

GET

Chiefs cornerback Jaylen Watson celebrates after returning an interception for a touchdown against Los Angeles.

Colts 20, Chiefs 17 September 25, 2022

Chiefs Lose Ugly

K.C. Defense Helps Colts' Matt Ryan Lead Game-Winning Drive

INDIANAPOLIS —

MATT RYAN KEPT THE FAITH SUNDAY.

As the 37-year-old quarterback looked around the huddle, he sensed his Indianapolis Colts teammates would find a way to make some big plays late. Eventually, with a little help from the Kansas City defense, they did.

Ryan capped a masterfully managed final drive by finding rookie Jelani Woods on a 12-yard touchdown pass with 24 seconds left for a 20-17 comeback win over the Chiefs. It was Ryan's first victory with the Colts — sealed by Rodney McLeod Jr.'s interception with 2 seconds to go.

"Sometimes you have a game where it's just not right and you have to tighten things up, but you can't be uptight," Ryan said, referring to last week's shutout loss at Jacksonville. "You have to be loose enough to believe we're going to make these plays."

While this one certainly wasn't pretty and, at times, was downright ugly, the Colts (1-1-1) still managed to snap a four-game winless streak that dated to last season's final two games. Indy looked listless in all four.

This time, the defense stymied Patrick Mahomes & Co., giving up just a field goal in the second half and two touchdowns following turnovers in Colts territory. The offense, meanwhile, did just enough to take advantage of some uncharacteristic Chiefs miscues.

And when it mattered most, Ryan was at his best. He finished 27 of 37 for 222 yards despite getting sacked five times and losing two fumbles. And he found Woods twice for touchdowns. The first gave Indy its first lead of the season and the second one, wrestled away by Woods, gave Indy the win.

"That's the player we expect Jelani to be," coach Frank Reich said. "He's a big man and he's fast. You could see his growth in the offseason and during training camp. He's just continued to get better."

The Chiefs (2-1) helped out, too.

An unsportsmanlike conduct call on defensive tackle Chris Jones following a third-down sack extended Indy's final drive with less than five minutes to play. Ryan wasn't sure what drew the penalty. Referee Shawn Smith later explained it was for abusive language.

Chiefs kicker Matt Ammendola missed an extra point in the first half and a 34-yard field goal just before Ryan led the decisive drive. Ammendola was replacing an injured Harrison Butker.

Plus there was a fake field goal that resulted in a turnover on downs.

Still, the Chiefs appeared to be in control after Clyde Edwards-Helaire's 1-yard TD run and Travis Kelce's 2-point conversion catch made it 14-10 late in the first half.

But after three third-quarter field goals gave the Chiefs a 17-13 lead, they didn't score again and couldn't stop the Colts on the final 16-play, 76-yard drive that took nearly 8 1/2 minutes. Mahomes then threw his first interception of the season.

"Whenever you're playing a tough game like this one, you have to execute at a high level," Mahomes said. "Our schedule gets no easier, so we have to get better quickly. If we don't, the Ls are going to start piling up."

Colts running back Jonathan Taylor is lifted up by Kansas City linebacker Nick Bolton (32) and safety Bryan Cook.

Chiefs 41, Buccaneers 31 October 2, 2022

Bounceback Statement

Chiefs Show Their Best Side; Mahomes Upstages Tom Brady in Dominant Victory

TAMPA, Fla. —

PATRICK MAHOMES HAD ALL THE ANSWERS FOR SOLVING TAMPA BAY'S stingy defense, winning his latest matchup against Tom Brady in the stadium where the seven-time Super Bowl winner dealt him one of his most disappointing losses.

Mahomes threw for 249 yards and three touchdowns, including an electrifying jump pass to Clyde Edwards-Helaire, to lead the Chiefs to a 41-31 victory over the Buccaneers on Sunday night.

Playing at sold out Raymond James Stadium only four days after Hurricane Ian ravaged portions of Florida, Mahomes had TD throws of 16 yards to Travis Kelce, 1 yard to Edwards-Helaire and 10 yards to Jody Fortson while making NFL history by reaching 20,000 yards passing faster than anyone else.

Edwards-Helaire and tight end Noah Gray rushed for TDs for the Chiefs (3-1), who won the first meeting between Mahomes and Brady since Tampa Bay's 31-9 rout of Kansas City in the Super Bowl — also played at Raymond James Stadium — two seasons ago.

"When I came into the stadium I realized that I hadn't been here and the bad taste I had last time came into effect," Mahomes said. "But it's still not a playoff game. It's a regular-season game, which is important. That Super Bowl will always leave a bad taste for me."

The short pass to Edwards-Helaire was Mahomes at his improvisational best: He escaped two defenders, did a 360-degree spin move and flipped the ball over a crowd to the running back in the back of the end zone.

"I was able to use my speed, my little bit of speed, to get around the edge there. I was gonna run for it, but they kind of flew around me," Mahomes said. "I realized I wasn't going to make it and I saw Clyde, so I kind of flicked it up to him."

Brady noted it's fun watching Mahomes, unless he's on the opposing sideline.

"I love seeing Patrick play. ... unfortunately, we're on the wrong end of it tonight," said Brady, who's 1-2 against the Chiefs quarterback since joining the Bucs in 2020 after two decades with the New England Patriots.

Brady completed 39 of 52 passes for 385 yards and three TDs without an interception for Tampa Bay (2-2). The Bucs, however, played from behind the whole night after rookie Rachaad White fumbled the opening kickoff and Mahomes threw his TD pass to Kelce two plays later.

The Chiefs also got into the end zone on three of their next four possessions, with Mahomes repeatedly shredding the Tampa Bay defense with pinpoint passes and Edwards-Helaire and Isiah Pacheco taking turns running the ball effectively.

"It's a team sport. We didn't play great on offense. We didn't help (the defense) much, either," Brady said.

Chiefs cornerback L'Jarius Sneed sacked Brady, forcing a fumble that Mahomes turned into Gray's TD, with the tight end taking a direct snap from center on the 1-yard plunge that put Kansas City up 28-10.

Brady threw TD passes of 13 yards and 1 yard to Mike Evans, who returned from serving a one-game suspension for his role in a on-field brawl at New Orleans two weeks ago.

Chiefs receiver JuJu Smith-Schuster gets ahead of Tampa Bay Buccaneers cornerback Carlton Davis III during the second half.

Travis Kelce crosses the goal line on a first-half touchdown reception.

The Jet

McKinnon's Contribution to Chiefs Outsized at First Glance

HE ANSWERS TO THE NICKNAME JET, CONFESSES TO HAVING "LITTLE MAN" syndrome and has a high-pitched voice — constantly imitated by his teammates and coach — that would make a high school freshman blush.

But Jerick McKinnon, the Chiefs' diminutive running back, has also made an outsized contribution as something of a quarterback helper. He caught nine touchdown passes during the regular season to tie the Hall of Famer Marshall Faulk's 2001 mark for scoring receptions by a running back.

"He just finds a way to get in the end zone," Kansas City quarterback Patrick Mahomes said. "A lot of those things he's not the first read, he's not the second read. He's able to just be in the right spot at the right time whenever I need to hit a check down, I can get it to him and then he makes the most of it by getting into the end zone."

Perhaps the best example of McKinnon's savvy came in a December game against the Denver Broncos, when Mahomes was flushed from the pocket and McKinnon shot ahead of a defender who keyed in on the quarterback. Mahomes quickly dished a no-look pass that McKinnon took 56 yards for a touchdown.

At 5-foot-9 and 216 pounds, McKinnon has also been a shockingly effective blocker, a skill that may help fend off the Bengals' defense in Sunday's A.F.C. championship game with Mahomes nursing a sprained right ankle. McKinnon, a 30-year-old journeyman, was selected as a playoff captain by his teammates because of his good humor and professionalism.

"It's not like he's looking for the glory or the praise," Mahomes said. "He just comes to work every single day with a smile on his face and he brings the energy. You ask anybody in the locker room, and he's probably one of, if not the favorite guy in the locker room."

Kansas City Coach Andy Reid said McKinnon had fulfilled the role of "big brother" for a team that is stacked with rookies and second- or third-year pros.

"He's got the high-pitched voice," Reid said. "Everybody thinks the world of him and loves him."

McKinnon's Kevin Hart-like high-octave patter earned him a turn on a Reddit thread about the least intimidating voices in the N.F.L. The fellow running back Clyde Edwards-Helaire's impersonation of McKinnon is the gold standard inside the Kansas City practice facility.

McKinnon has taken the long path to a breakout season. A third-round selection of the Minnesota Vikings in 2014, he spent four years as a backup before signing a four-year, $30 million deal with San Francisco in 2018. That year, McKinnon tore an anterior cruciate ligament, an injury that kept him from playing until 2020. He did not have many options left when Kansas City offered him a one-year deal before last season.

Reid says McKinnon's background as a quarterback at Georgia Southern University allows him to see the whole field and use his intuition to feel for where he needs to be as a play unfolds.

"He kind of knows how the game works as a whole," Reid said. "I think that helps him in the run game — knowing how gaps are set up, knowing how secondaries fill for the run. And on top of all that he can catch the ball."

Running back Jerick McKinnon proved that his versatility could be key to a Super Bowl run for Kansas City.

Chiefs 30, Raiders 29   October 10, 2022

Wild Times, Familiar Ending

After 17-Point First-Half Deficit, Chiefs Turn Game on its Head and Storm Back

KANSAS CITY, Mo. —

THE KANSAS CITY CHIEFS HEADED OFF TO THE LOCKER ROOM FACING A BIG hole against the Las Vegas Raiders on Monday night, everything from the big plays to the officiating calls going the way of their longtime AFC West rivals.

One call in particular lit a fire under them.

It was a dubious penalty on Chiefs defensive tackle Chris Jones for roughing Raiders quarterback Derek Carr, and nobody in the Kansas City locker room could believe it. But rather than stew over it, or lament their 10-point deficit, Patrick Mahomes and the rest of the Chiefs used it as motivation to storm from behind for the 30-29 victory.

"There was anger just about how we had played up to that point," said Mahomes, who threw four touchdown passes to tight end Travis Kelce. "We needed everybody to go out there and take the fight to them."

The Raiders still had a chance when Davante Adams, who earlier had hauled in a 58-yard touchdown catch, added a 48-yarder with 4:29 to go. It came after Kelce's final touchdown catch, when Kansas City failed on a 2-point try that left the score 30-23. But rather than kick a tying extra point, Raiders coach Josh McDaniels also went for 2.

Josh Jacobs, who had shredded the Chiefs defense all night, was stuffed at the goal line.

The Raiders got the ball back one last time with 2:29 left, and a long third-down pass to Adams down the Kansas City sideline appeared to get them in field-goal range. But the play was reviewed and Adams failed to get both feet in bounds, and Carr threw incomplete on fourth-and-1 with 47 seconds left before the Chiefs ran out the clock.

"We didn't fall apart on each other," Chiefs safety Justin Reid said. "We battled through adversity."

Carr finished with 241 yards passing, and Jacobs ran for 133 yards and a score, as the Raiders lost to the Chiefs (4-1) for the fourth straight time. Daniel Carlson was 3 for 3 on field goals, extending his streak to 38 in a row.

"We had a chance," Daniels said. "We just didn't make one or two plays there at the end to finish it."

The game of twists and turns began with the Raiders failing to score on their opening drive for the first time all season. They made up for it on the next one.

Facing fourth-and-inches in their own territory, McDaniels sent his offense back on the field. But rather than run Jacobs up the middle, or sneak with Carr, he aired it out to Adams, who ran past Rashad Fenton for the 58-yard TD catch.

It was 17-0 when Kelce finally reached the end zone for the Chiefs, but it appeared as if the momentum had turned when Jones stripped Carr from behind and landed him. But despite the ball clearly coming out, and the Pro Bowl defensive tackle coming away with it, referee Carl Cheffers threw a penalty flag and called Jones for roughing the passer.

Chiefs coach Andy Reid stormed off the sideline to argue. And after the teams traded field goals in the final minutes, leaving the Raiders ahead 20-10, Reid cornered Cheffers and lit into him again as the teams headed to the locker room.

Chiefs safety Juan Thornhill breaks up a pass intended for Las Vegas receiver Mack Hollins.

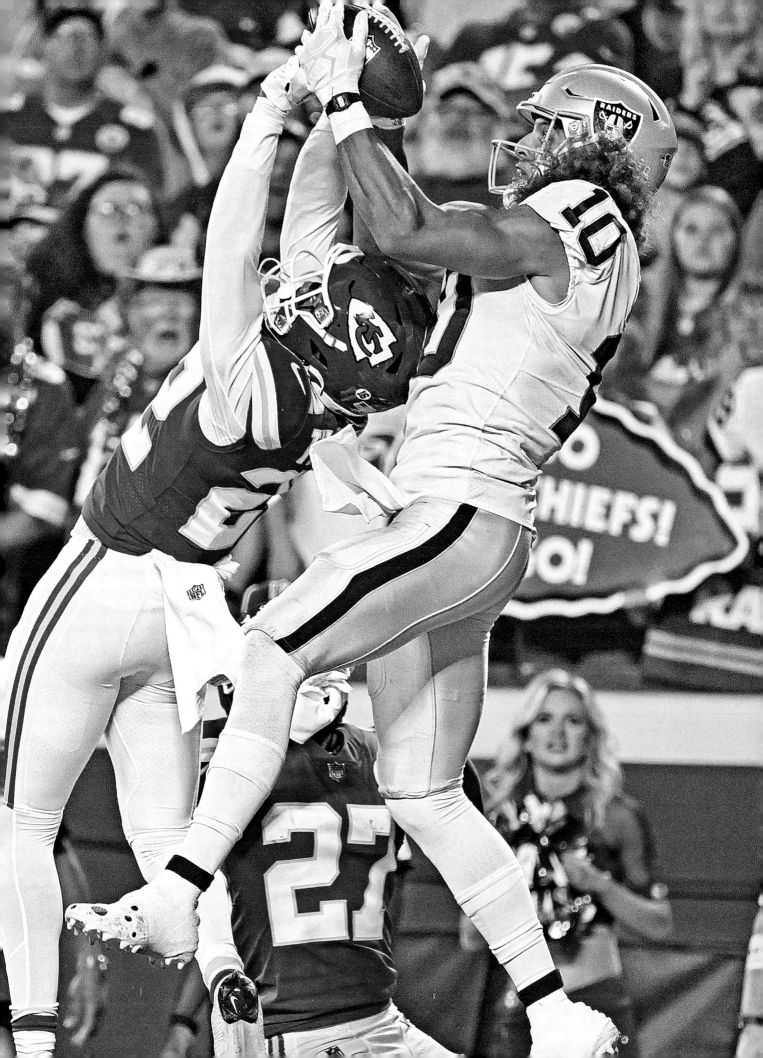

Kansas City linebacker
Nick Bolton celebrates
against the Raiders.

Bills 24, Chiefs 20   October 16, 2022

Upstaged in Showdown

Bills' Allen Outduels Mahomes in Playoff Rematch

KANSAS CITY, Mo. —

VON MILLER HAD JUST FINISHED TALKING ABOUT THE IMPORTANCE OF THE Buffalo Bills beating the Kansas City Chiefs at Arrowhead Stadium when he stopped in the hallway outside the visiting locker room and grabbed Josh Allen in a hug.

The Bills quarterback was masterful again on Sunday.

This time, it was in a winning effort.

Allen threw for 329 yards and three touchdowns, including the go-ahead toss to Dawson Knox with 1:04 left, and the Bills held on for a 24-20 victory to exact a measure of revenge for their epic overtime loss to Patrick Mahomes and the Chiefs in last year's playoffs.

"I've come to this stadium a whole bunch of times. Been at this same podium. But I ain't have many smiles," Miller said. "It just feels so good to go out there with my teammates, to work toward something like this and come out on top."

Stefon Diggs had 10 catches for 148 yards and a touchdown, and Gabe Davis also had a TD catch after torching Kansas City for four of them in January, as the Bills (5-1) won in the same place their season had ended the past two seasons.

It was the divisional round in January. It was the AFC championship game the year before that.

"Nothing we did last year translates to what we're doing this year," Allen said with a shrug. "What happened in the past, that's where it is. All we can do is focus on the next one. Today was the next one."

For a moment, it looked as if it could be the next heartbreak.

The Chiefs got the ball back after Knox's touchdown with plenty of time left. But after Mahomes misfired on first down, Buffalo cornerback Taron Johnson jumped his pass to Skyy Moore and picked him off with 51 seconds left.

The Bills ran out the clock from there.

"It was a great battle. You love these games," Chiefs coach Andy Reid said. "You just don't want to be sitting on this end of it. But you love the competition and the way the guys get after it."

Mahomes finished with 338 yards passing to go with two touchdowns and two interceptions.

The down-to-the-wire nail-biter was a fitting follow-up to their playoff game, when the teams combined to score 25 points in the final two minutes of regulation, and the Chiefs (4-2) won it on the first possession of overtime.

The teams scored on their final six possessions that night, and they picked up Sunday right where they left off — with a small caveat. The Bills and Chiefs both marched the length of the field in the first quarter, chewing up defenses that looked downright lost, only to turn the ball over when they reached the red zone.

Mahomes, at his improvisational best, stayed alive long enough in a collapsing pocket to find Smith-Schuster for a 42-yard TD reception. And after the Bills blew another red-zone opportunity, when Allen threw incomplete on fourth-and-goal at Kansas City's 3, Buffalo answered with a touchdown drive in the final minute of the half.

Bills quarterback Josh Allen hurdles Kansas City safety Justin Reid.

Chiefs 44, 49ers 23 October 23, 2022

K.C. Snaps Out of Funk

Chiefs Fall Behind 49ers Early Before Rallying Emphatically

SANTA CLARA, Calif. —

FALLING INTO AN EARLY HOLE WAS JUST WHAT THE KANSAS CITY CHIEFS needed to get going.

Patrick Mahomes threw for 423 yards and three touchdowns to rally Kansas City back from another double-digit deficit in the Chiefs' 44-23 victory over the San Francisco 49ers on Sunday.

"I think we like playing when we're down," defensive lineman Chris Jones said. "I guess we like challenging ourselves at this point. No one got rattled. We came together as a team."

Mahomes got off to a rough start in this Super Bowl rematch with his early interception putting Kansas City (5-2) in a 10-0 hole but that once again proved to be no problem as he led the Chiefs to touchdowns on six of the next seven drives.

Mecole Hardman scored on two TD runs and an 8-yard catch, Justin Watson caught a 4-yard TD and JuJu Smith-Schuster finished it off with a 45 yard catch and run. Clyde Edwards-Helaire also scored on a 16-yard run as the Chiefs had their most productive offensive game of the season.

"To go out against defense like this and show that we can still be explosive and have those big plays, I think that will bode well for us as the season goes on and people don't know where it's going to come from," Mahomes said.

The comeback improved Kansas City to 13-9 with Mahomes when falling behind by at least 10 points with the most memorable coming in a Super Bowl win over the 49ers (3-4) following the 2019 season.

The Niners dropped back-to-back games despite getting a boost from the addition this week of running back Christian McCaffrey, who had 62 yards on 10 scrimmage touches in his San Francisco debut.

But San Francisco settled for three field goals and came up empty on another chance when Jimmy Garoppolo threw an interception at the goal line before Kansas City ran away with it in the second half.

"We definitely had our chances," defensive end Nick Bosa said. "It's a great team and we gave them too many easy ones."

The Chiefs took control with back-to-back touchdown drives to start the second half. They started the opening drive of the third quarter at the San Francisco 33 following a 48-yard kick return by Isiah Pacheco and a personal foul on Jauan Jennings. Edwards-Helaire scored three players later to make it 21-13.

Kansas City made it 28-13 when Mahomes found Watson for the TD one play after Jerick McKinnon gained 34 yards on a third-and-20 screen pass.

"Once the defense gets a stop and once you're on one, it's like you're playing Madden," Smith-Schuster said. "They have the X-factor on the quarterback. They had one on Pat today. He was on fire."

Mahomes then answered a TD pass from Garoppolo to George Kittle by hitting Marquez Valdes-Scantling on a 57-yard pass on third-and-11 to set up Hardman's second TD run.

Mahomes found Smith-Schuster on another third down play for the final TD.

JuJu Smith-Schuster crosses the goal line to score, completing a 45-yard touchdown reception from Patrick Mahomes.

Chiefs receiver Mecole Hardman scores a touchdown against the 49ers.

Chiefs 20, Titans 17 (OT)   November 6, 2022

Sandlot Football

Mahomes Improvises Enough to Lead Chiefs Past Titans in Overtime

KANSAS CITY, Mo. —

PATRICK MAHOMES WAS PROBABLY HAVING FLASHBACKS SUNDAY NIGHT TO his days at Texas Tech, when he would scramble around like a kid playing sandlot football while routinely throwing the ball 60-plus times in a game.

The Chiefs needed all of it — every run, every throw, every yard — to rally past the Tennessee Titans.

Mahomes finished 43 of 68 for 446 yards and a touchdown, and he ran for the tying score and 2-point conversion late in the fourth quarter, before Harrison Butker atoned for two earlier misses by drilling the go-ahead field goal in overtime and lifting the Chiefs to the 20-17 victory.

"I did not know I threw that many," Mahomes said with a smile, "but yeah, Texas Tech, I threw a couple, so I'm able to do it."

Chiefs coach Andy Reid improved to 21-3 coming off a bye by beating a franchise that has long been his nemesis. He was just 2-9 against the Titans — heck, Reid has three wins against the Chiefs — including a 27-3 loss in Nashville last year.

It was only the second win for Kansas City (6-2) in its last seven games against the Titans.

"You have to be able to win a game like that," Reid said, "where everything isn't just perfect, and your emotions are up and down and you have to fight through. We were so close on so many plays. Step up and let's go."

Things were spiraling toward another disappointment the way Derrick Henry was chewing up yardage against the Kansas City defense, and the way the Titans (5-3) were shutting down Mahomes and Co. into the fourth quarter.

Indeed, the Chiefs were trailing 17-9 and time was running out when they took over at their own 7-yard line. But in vintage Mahomes fashion, he willed his team downfield. His 20-yard scramble on third-and-17 kept the drive going, and his third-and-9 touchdown scramble along with his 2-point conversion run knotted the game with 2:56 to go.

After the Chiefs won the overtime coin toss, the Titans nearly stopped them, only for Noah Gray to make a nifty third-down catch. Then, Mahomes hit JuJu Smith-Schuster on fourth down to keep the drive alive — and the clock moving.

Butker drilled his 28-yarder to give Kansas City the lead with 4:04 left in overtime.

The Chiefs proceeded to stuff Henry, then sacked Titans rookie Malik Willis on back-to-back plays, before batting down his fourth-down throw to end the game and send fireworks flying into the sky above Arrowhead Stadium.

"When you get to those end-of-the-game situations," Mahomes said, "you have to try to go out there and make it happen."

Henry finished with 115 yards rushing and two touchdowns for the Titans. But he didn't get a whole lot of help from Willis, who got his second start in place of the injured Ryan Tannehill, and was just 5 of 16 for 80 yards.

"I'm very disappointed. I feel terrible for the players," Titans coach Mike Vrabel said. "They compete, and put so much into this, and play through pain and discomfort and any situation."

Kansas City kicker Harrison Butker knocks a field goal through against the Titans.

Patrick Mahomes scrambles for yardage in a 20-17 win over the Titans at Arrowhead Stadium.

Kansas City tight end
Noah Gray catches a
pass against Tennessee
cornerback Roger
McCreary.

Frank Clark and Chris Jones

Wired for the Spotlight

Defensive Linemen Step up Like Champions for Kansas City

KANSAS CITY CHIEFS DEFENSIVE END FRANK CLARK HAS NO SIMPLE explanation for why he becomes one of the NFL's all-time great pass-rushers in the postseason. But he readily acknowledges that it does happen.

"It just all comes together at that point," Clark said after he logged 1.5 sacks in the AFC Championship Game victory over the Cincinnati Bengals. "I kind of get a little more freedom in the postseason. It's win or go home. When you've got that mindset as a player and when you've got that mindset as a coach ... that's where it comes from. When I get to the postseason, I get that nod from Coach [Andy] Reid. It's like, 'Go ahead and do your thing.'

"There's a reason they [brought] me here. I told the guys [the day before the game] I was going to set the tone from the start of the game to the end of the game."

Counting the sack Clark had in the Chiefs' divisional round playoff win over the Jacksonville Jaguars, he's now third on the NFL's career postseason list with 13.5. With one sack in Super Bowl LVII against the Philadelphia Eagles on Feb. 12, he would tie Hall of Famer Bruce Smith for second place. He would tie the all-time leader, Willie McGinest, with 2.5 sacks.

Clark isn't the only Chiefs pass-rusher carving out a postseason legacy for himself. Chris Jones had a game for the ages against the Bengals. Though he was blocked by two players on a large percentage of plays, Jones still had two sacks, 10 pressures and five hits on quarterback Joe Burrow.

Jones had been preparing for a playoff rematch against the Bengals ever since he missed on some sack attempts on Burrow in last year's AFC Championship Game, all of which were key plays in the Bengals' overtime win.

"My whole offseason was dedicated to this game," Jones said. "I missed a few big plays last year. They were able to move forward [to the Super Bowl] and I put that on my shoulders. I dedicated my whole offseason to making sure when the moment came for me again that I'd answer the call."

Jones' performance against the Bengals was hardly a breakout -- he knocked down three passes in the Chiefs' Super Bowl LIV win over the San Francisco 49ers -- but the seven-year vet did reach a milestone.

Despite two years with 15.5 sacks, including this season, and 65 career sacks in the regular season, Jones had been shut out in sacks in 13 career postseason games. Until the AFC Championship Game.

"I personally do not care about sacks in the playoffs," Jones said. "My job is to make sure that I play hard, I play physical and [help] my teammates around me make plays, whether it's taking the double team the whole game or whether it's getting the one-on-one and winning.

"Me being doubled means the guys around me are able to get single blocks and I'm able to open up the game for a lot of individuals on the line of scrimmage. If you take the me out of it and the selfish aspect out of it, you're a friend of your teammates and it's not meant for you to make all the sacks all the time, as much as I'd love to. Sometimes it's about you freeing up other players so they can excel."

Jones' performance against the Bengals is the only playoff game since the pass rush win rate statistic was introduced in 2017 in which at least 80% of a player's rushes came against a double team and the player went on to record multiple sacks.

Chiefs defensive tackle Chris Jones (95) and defensive end Frank Clark look on during a game against Denver.

Chiefs defensive end Frank Clark (55) celebrates a sack of Bengals quarterback Joe Burrow with teammates George Karlaftis (56) and Justin Reid during the AFC Championship in January.

Chiefs 27, Jaguars 17 November 13, 2022

Jaguars Outshined

Mahomes Throws Four TDs as Chiefs Throttle Jaguars

KANSAS CITY, Mo. —

PATRICK MAHOMES AND THE KANSAS CITY CHIEFS WERE ROLLING THROUGH
the Jaguars defense when Jacksonville safety Andre Cisco delivered a helmet-to-helmet blow that left wide receiver JuJu Smith-Schuster motionless on the turf.

Rather than slow down the Chiefs, the questionable hit infuriated them.

Mahomes threw for 331 yards with touchdown passes to four different receivers, and the Kansas City offense piled up nearly 500 yards despite three turnovers in a 27-17 victory Sunday.

"My reaction, I was angry. I was kind of mad," said Chiefs wide receiver Kadarius Toney, who had one of the touchdown catches. "I don't like no dirty plays. I felt like it kind of gave the team a boost, gave us something to really put us on our back. It gave us something to play for, you could say."

Toney, who was acquired a couple of week ago from the Giants, had 33 yards rushing to go with four catches for 57 yards and his first NFL touchdown reception. Travis Kelce, Marquez Valdes-Scantling and Noah Gray also had touchdown catches, and Isiah Pacheco ran for 82 yards as the Chiefs (7-2) beat the Jaguars (3-7) for the sixth straight time. Kansas City took over the best record in the AFC.

"They gave us all we could handle," Chiefs coach Andy Reid said, "and it wound up being a good game at the end."

Trevor Lawrence threw for 259 yards and two touchdowns, both to Christian Kirk, who finished with nine catches for 105 yards for the Jaguars. Zay Jones also had eight catches for 68 yards while Travis Etienne ran for 45 yards.

"It's tough to win games in general when you don't take advantage of opportunities, especially against a really good team," Lawrence said. "Too many missed opportunities early. We still had our chances at the end, but we didn't make the plays."

The Jaguars became the first team in five years to recover an onside kick to open the game, but their offense squandered the opportunity — and several more. They punted five times and missed a field goal on their first six possessions.

The Chiefs had no such trouble reaching the end zone.

Mahomes, trying to become the third quarterback in NFL history with three straight 400-yard passing games, had 191 by halftime. That included the first NFL touchdown reception for Toney, the injury-prone former first-round draft pick who the Chiefs acquired in a trade with the Giants a couple of weeks ago.

"It just felt electric," Toney said. "I was too close to the sideline when I caught it, and I was just excited. I was like, 'Oh, I got to get in there, somehow, some way.' But it was electric."

Later in the half, Smith-Schuster was hit by Cisco while catching a pass over the middle, leaving his hands momentarily frozen.

Officials initially threw a flag for the helmet-to-helmet hit on a defenseless receiver, but referee Brad Rogers said that the official's determined Cisco was leading with his shoulder and picked up the flag.

"He was in a defenseless posture," Rogers said, "but they didn't feel that there was any use-of-helmet foul on that."

Kansas City tight end Travis Kelce (left) celebrates a touchdown with guard Trey Smith against the Jaguars.

Chiefs receiver Kadarius Toney leaps high to make a catch over Jacksonville cornerback Montaric Brown for a 22-yard gain in the third quarter.

Chiefs 30, Chargers 27 November 20, 2022

Still Best in the West

Kelce Snags Three Scores — Including Game-Winner —As Chiefs Upend Chargers

INGLEWOOD, Calif. —

PATRICK MAHOMES AND TRAVIS KELCE ENDED UP PUTTING ON A performance that made The Fonz proud.

Mahomes connected with Kelce for three touchdowns — including the go-ahead score with 31 seconds remaining — as the Kansas City Chiefs rallied past the Los Angeles Chargers 30-27 on Sunday night to stay atop the AFC.

Mahomes met Emmy Award-winning actor Henry Winkler before the game. Winkler, who played Fonzie for 12 seasons on the iconic television show "Happy Days", received a signed jersey on the sideline. Kelce got in the act by wearing a t-shirt before the game that had a picture of The Fonz and said "Football. Family. Fonzie".

When Mahomes and the Chiefs got the ball at the KC 25-yard line with 1:46 remaining, he had his usual cool and calm presence.

"When I went in the huddle, it was let's just do it. Everyone had the mindset of take it one play at a time and get it when it counts," said Mahomes, completed 20 of 34 passes for 329 yards.

After the Chargers had pulled ahead 27-23 on Justin Herbert's 6-yard touchdown pass to Joshua Palmer with 1:46 left, Mahomes directed a six-play, 75-yard drive that took just 1:15.

It was the 11th time in the regular-season that Mahomes had a game-winning drive in the fourth quarter.

Despite missing two receivers due to injuries, he completed 3 of 4 for 48 yards on the drive and scrambled twice for an additional 22.

The Chiefs also benefitted from a third-down holding call on Chargers' safety Derwin James after an incomplete pass.

After a 16-yard run by Mahomes and Kansas City timeout, Mahomes hit Kelce on a short crossing route that Kelce took to the end zone for a 17-yard touchdown,

"We didn't have our full arsenal of weapons. I was ready for the matchup," said Kelce, who had six catches for 115 yards. "I knew they were going to play man-to-man and Patrick was going to look for me when it was 1-on-1. I was able to finish the game off on a positive note."

Herbert and the Chargers had one final chance, but Nick Bolton intercepted a deflected pass to seal it for the Chiefs (8-2), who swept the season series from Los Angeles (5-5) and took a three-game lead in the AFC West.

It is the third straight year the Chargers have had a late lead at home against the Chiefs and were unable to finish.

"You should be frustrated. To not beat those guys is disappointing because we felt like our level was good enough to win, but we didn't finish plays in that fourth quarter to get it done," Chargers coach Brandon Staley said after Los Angeles lost its second straight to fall to 5-5.

With a one-game lead over four teams in the conference, Kansas City is in position to claim home-field advantage throughout the playoffs.

Chiefs rookie Isiah Pacheco rushed for a career-high 107 yards.

Travis Kelce, celebrates after scoring a touchdown during the fourth quarter against the Chargers.

Travis Kelce runs into the end zone for the game-winning touchdown late in the fourth quarter against Los Angeles.

Chiefs 26, Rams 10 November 27, 2022

Big Win, Muted Celebration

Mistakes Pile Up Despite Decisive Victory over Defending Super Bowl Champs

KANSAS CITY, Mo. —
ANDY REID LAMENTED MORE PROBLEMS WITH THE KANSAS CITY CHIEFS PUNT
return unit. JuJu Smith-Schuster regretted their many failures in the red zone. Patrick Mahomes bemoaned "the one dumb play I make every game."

So much for celebrating a 26-10 victory Sunday over the beat-up Los Angeles Rams.

Sure, the Chiefs were pleased by Mahomes throwing for 320 yards and a touchdown, and the hard yardage Isiah Pacheco gained on the ground eventually netted him a score. And they were thrilled with the performance of their defense, which frustrated fill-in quarterback Bryce Perkins and shut down the Rams ground game.

But the Chiefs also made plenty of mistakes, including an interception by Mahomes in the end zone in the fourth quarter — that dumb play he referenced — and red-zone woes that led to four field goals by Harrison Butker.

"Got to do a little better in the red zone. That's a place where we're normally pretty good," Reid said. "We were off a tick tonight. We'll get back to the drawing board and take care of that."

It didn't matter against the Rams, who have lost five straight for the first time under Sean McVay.

It might matter against the Bengals next week. And down the stretch in the pursuit of the AFC's top seed.

"You like the win but we have a lot to get better at," Mahomes said, "especially me."

Still, the Chiefs (9-2) have won six of the last seven against Los Angeles, and they exacted a measure of revenge for that lone defeat, when then-Rams quarterback Jared Goff threw a late TD pass to win a 54-51 thriller in November 2018.

Playing without Matthew Stafford, who remained in the concussion protocol, the Rams (3-8) struggled to move the chains behind Perkins, a career backup making his first start. He made a couple of nice plays with his legs but threw for just 100 yards with a touchdown pass and two interceptions.

"It's hard to say that you're running anything that resembles anything close to your offense and what you envisioned it to be," Rams coach Sean McVay said. "There's a lot of challenges based on what guys know and their skill sets."

The Rams' losing streak and their record through 11 games matches the 1987 Giants for the worst among defending Super Bowl champs, though New York's dismal start came amid a strike resulting in the use of replacement players.

The Rams certainly looked like a team playing without its starting quarterback, top two wide receivers and two starting offensive linemen — all out with injuries Sunday. They scrapped just to get positive yardage on every snap, and that's only when they managed to get the play off in time or didn't have to waste a timeout.

The Chiefs didn't penalize them early for their many miscues, though defensive tackle Chris Jones did pick up his 10th sack of the season, triggering a $1.25 million incentive. Kansas City instead marched methodically down field only to twice settle for field goals, leaving the woebegone Rams surprisingly within 13-3 lead at intermission.

Chiefs running back Isiah Pacheco makes a catch against the Rams in the second half of a 26-10 win.

Kansas City running back Jerick McKinnon attempts to avoid a tackle by Rams safety Taylor Rapp.

Bengals 27, Chiefs 24 December 4, 2022

Burrow Myth Grows

Bengals Quarterback Earns Third Career Win Over Kansas City

CINCINNATI —

JOE BURROW GOT A HUGE ASSIST FROM HIS DEFENSE IN ANOTHER RIVETING duel with Patrick Mahomes.

With the Chiefs leading Burrow's Bengals 24-20 early in in the fourth quarter on Sunday, Mahomes hooked up with Travis Kelce, who rumbled for a big gain. But while Bengals linebacker Germaine Pratt and other defenders were wrestling Kelce to the ground, Pratt forced the ball free and recovered the ensuing fumble.

Burrow took it from there, completing 6 of 7 passes during a 53-yard drive that he finished with a go-ahead 8-yard touchdown to backup running back Chris Evans. The Bengals' defense held Kansas City scoreless from there and Burrow closed out a 27-24 victory over the Chiefs.

"He's playing at an MVP level – absolutely," Bengals coach Zac Taylor said. "He gives us a lot of confidence."

The Bengals (8-4) have won four straight overall and their last three meetings with Kansas City (9-3) — all in the same calendar year. Cincinnati won on Jan. 2 to clinch the AFC North title. Four weeks later, the Bengals beat the Chiefs at Arrowhead Stadium in overtime — also by a 27-24 score — to reach the Super Bowl for the first time in 33 years.

This time, Burrow finished 25 of 31 with two touchdowns and ran in for a 4-yard score to get the Bengals on the board in the first quarter. He concluded his day by converting two third downs on passes to Ja'Marr Chase and Tee Higgins, allowing the Bengals to run out the clock.

"We left some points on the field, but we still find a way to win," Burrow said. "We've still got five weeks left. Let's keep this train rolling. This team knows what it takes to win these games. We've been there. It's December. It's time to separate ourselves."

Cincinnati running back Samaje Perine ran for a season-high 106 yards on 21 tough carries.

Mahomes was 16 for 27 for 223 yards and a touchdown and ran for another score. But the Chiefs fell short on their final possession when Joseph Ossai sacked Mahomes on third-and-3 from the Bengals 33, and Harrison Butker missed a 55-yard field goal wide right.

"We started off slow, we got back in the game, into the flow of things and (then) we had a turnover late and a missed kick," Mahomes said. "In the fourth quarter, those are the things that kind of bite you at the end."

Cincinnati led for the entire the first half and took a 14-10 advantage into the locker room.

Mahomes led Kansas City on two methodical third-quarter drives that ended in touchdowns — an 8-yard-run by Isiah Pacheco and a 3-yard scramble by the multi-talented QB — while the Bengals had to settle for a pair of field goals. That gave the Chiefs a 24-20 lead that held until the turnover and subsequent Cincinnati TD.

Chiefs head coach Andy Reid defended his decision to attempt a long field goal on the final possession that would have tied the game instead of keeping Mahomes on the field.

"If I don't think he's going to make that, I'm not going to do it," Reid said. "It's pretty simple. I feel like (Butker) has been in a good place, and we just have to execute it better all the way around."

Jerick McKinnon scores a touchdown during a 27-24 defeat at Cincinnati.

Andy Reid

Playing the Long Game

Ried Turned a Binder into a Hall of Fame Resumé

ANDY REID WAS AN UNKNOWN ASSISTANT IN GREEN BAY WHEN EAGLES owner Jeffrey Lurie took a chance on hiring Brett Favre's position coach to revive a struggling franchise in Philadelphia.

A newspaper headline greeted Reid's arrival with a headline that said: "Andy Who?"

Everybody knows his name now.

Reid won more games (130) than any coach in franchise history during his 14 seasons with the Eagles. He led Philadelphia to nine playoff appearances, six division titles and five NFC championship games. But Reid couldn't deliver a Super Bowl victory, losing to the New England Patriots after the 2004 season. For that reason, he was underappreciated by many fans and reporters in Philly.

Reid eventually lost his job after only his third losing season in 2012, and immediately landed in Kansas City. He finally hoisted that elusive Vince Lombardi Trophy with Patrick Mahomes and the Chiefs three years ago.

By that time, the Eagles had won their first Super Bowl under then-coach Doug Pederson, one of Reid's prized pupils.

Now, Reid and the Eagles are going head-to-head aiming for that second title. The Chiefs (16-3) vs. the Eagles (16-3) is one of the most-anticipated Super Bowl matchups in recent years.

Just don't expect the stoic Reid to get emotional about it.

"When you really cut to the chase on it, they're a really good football team and so, I think that's where the energy goes because really when it's kickoff, you're playing that team," Reid said Monday.

"It's the players that you're going against and the coaches and so the uniform (and) all, that's not where your mind's at. Your mind's at making sure you have a solid game plan and that you come out and you can perform to the best of our ability.

"That's, I think, where the major focus goes, and you try to — it doesn't matter who you're playing — you try to blank out all the hype that goes with the game. It's a pretty big game for everybody. ... It's a big, big deal. It's the Super Bowl. But you try to blank that out and make sure that you're getting the game plan — what really matters — together."

Nearly a quarter century since he walked into an interview with the Eagles armed with a 6-inch binder containing notes on how to build a winning team, Reid has amassed Hall of Fame credentials. He's led the Chiefs to nine playoff appearances, including seven consecutive division titles in 10 winning seasons. He's been to five straight AFC title games, winning three.

"It's a real testament to the job that general manager Brett Veach and Coach Reid have done over the last several years," Chiefs chairman Clark Hunt said after the team clinched the division last month.

"We obviously have a bunch of young players and we've got some new players, and Andy and his staff have done a tremendous job of incorporating them into the team. That's just part of the National Football League. They've really done a fantastic job, and I couldn't be prouder of them."

Reid is a no-nonsense, old-school coach who is respected and loved by his players. He rarely throws anyone under the bus. Part of the criticism he received from reporters in Philly was for his unwillingness to call anyone out and to always shoulder all the blame after losses and poor

Kansas City coach Andy Reid talks with quarterback Patrick Mahomes during a game against the Bengals in December.

performances. "I gotta do a better job" became a punch line.

He came across as robotic in news conferences, always opening with injuries before turning it over to reporters for questions by saying: "Time's yours."

At 64, Reid has become more of a lovable grandpa in Kansas City. He's known for wearing floral shirts and cracking jokes about his weight. Ask Reid how he plans to celebrate a victory and he'll say with a cheeseburger.

"I'm gonna go get the biggest cheeseburger you've ever seen!" Reid said after the Chiefs beat the 49ers in the Super Bowl on Feb. 2, 2020.

After a victory over the Seahawks on Dec. 24, Mahomes and All-Pro tight end Travis Kelce presented Reid with a cheeseburger inside a wrapped Nike shoe box as a Christmas gift.

Players in the locker room cheered and hollered.

Reid smiled and shouted: "May you all get a gift as great as this."

Another Lombardi trophy would be the best present of all.

Andy Reid opens a giant cheesburger, gifted to him by Patrick Mahomes and Travis Kelce, after a win over Seattle in December.

Chiefs 34, Broncos 28 December 11, 2022

Off Day No Problem in the End

Mahomes Makes Uncharacteristic Mistakes but Chiefs Find Way Past Broncos

DENVER —

L'JARIUS SNEED INTERCEPTED BRONCOS BACKUP QUARTERBACK BRETT Rypien late in the fourth quarter, Patrick Mahomes atoned for a three-interception day by leading Kansas City on a clock-chewing drive, and the Chiefs held on for a 34-28 win on Sunday over Denver, which lost QB Russell Wilson to a concussion.

The Chiefs (10-3) extended their dominance of Denver with their 14th consecutive win over the Broncos (3-10), who made a game of it by scoring three touchdowns in a 3 1/2-minute stretch spanning halftime after falling behind 27-0.

Mahomes threw for 352 yards and three touchdowns, including a no-look hook pass on one of Jerick McKinnon's two TD receptions.

Jerry Jeudy caught three touchdown passes for Denver, the last one from Rypien after Wilson took a hard hit on a 14-yard scramble to the Kansas City 2 early in the fourth quarter. Wilson was escorted off the field and the Broncos ruled him out with a concussion shortly thereafter.

The Chiefs reached double digits in wins for the eighth straight season and inched closer to winning their seventh consecutive AFC West crown. A Chargers loss Sunday night to the Dolphins would clinch the division for Kansas City, which hasn't lost to Denver since 2015.

The Broncos lost their fifth straight game. They have lost eight straight when hosting Kansas City. Denver also has lost eight consecutive AFC West games for the first time since divisional play began with the 1970 AFL-NFL merger.

After a pair of Kansas City field goals, Mahomes was scrambling for the first down on third-and-2 when he shook defensive lineman D.J. Jones and flung a pass across his body to a wide-open McKinnon, who raced down Denver's dejected sideline for a 56-yard touchdown and a 13-0 lead.

Mahomes and McKinnon connected on a 10-yard TD on Kansas City's next possession. At that point, Mahomes had 224 passing yards to Wilson's 33.

On fourth-and-2 at his own 45-yard line, Wilson tried to throw a screen pass to Brandon Johnson but didn't get it high enough. Linebacker Willie Gay deflected the throw, corralled the ball in his left hand and stiff-armed Wilson with his right, sending him tumbling as he raced 47 yards for the touchdown.

That put the Chiefs in charge at 27-0 with 4:32 left in the half.

Jeudy caught his first two touchdown passes, from 18 and 5 yards out, after Mahomes uncharacteristically threw interceptions — to Josey Jewell and Patrick Surtain II — on consecutive possessions, making it 27-14 at the half.

On the opening drive after halftime, running back Marlon Mack caught a short pass from Wilson and raced 66 yards for the end zone to pull Denver within 27-21. Mahomes countered with a 4-yard TD strike to JuJu Smith-Schuster.

Jeudy's third TD came with 10:49 left.

JuJu Smith-Schuster celebrates a touchdown reception against the Broncos in December.

Jerick McKinnon dives over the Denver defense into the end zone.

Chiefs 30, Texans 24 (OT)   December 18, 2022

Texans Eventually Dispatched

Chiefs Celebrate AFC West Title With Overtime Victory

HOUSTON —

WEARING SHIRTS THAT READ "CONQUERED THE WEST" AND BASEBALL caps commemorating their AFC West title, the Kansas City Chiefs celebrated winning the division for a seventh straight season after outlasting the Houston Texans in overtime Sunday.

Amid the jubilation, their star quarterback was quick to point out the feat was only the beginning of what they hope to do this season.

"When we start every season, the first thing we get told when we first walk in is let's win the AFC West," Patrick Mahomes said. "That's our first goal ... (and) we accomplished our first goal."

Jerick McKinnon had a 26-yard touchdown run in overtime and the Chiefs got three touchdowns from Mahomes in the 30-24 win.

The Chiefs (11-3) got the ball first in overtime but had to punt it away after Mahomes was sacked by Blake Cashman on third down. Texans quarterback Davis Mills fumbled on a scramble on Houston's first play, and it was recovered by Kansas City's Willie Gay on the Texans' 26.

McKinnon, who also had a TD reception, dashed untouched into the end zone on the next play.

He said Mahomes reminded him before the play to keep two hands on the ball.

"I said: 'I'm about to score,'" McKinnon said. "Juju (Smith-Schuster) looked at me and said: 'I've got your block, bro. Just find me when you get out there'. And it worked out exactly like that."

Houston (1-12-1) tied it at 24 on a 29-yard field goal with about five minutes to go in the fourth quarter. The Chiefs had a chance to win it in regulation, but Harrison Butker's 51-yard attempt was wide right.

Kansas City overcame two turnovers and a season-high 102 penalty yards to win for the seventh time in eight games.

Mills threw for 121 yards and two touchdowns sharing time at quarterback with Jeff Driskel. The Texans dropped their ninth straight game for their longest skid since losing the final 14 games of the 2013 season.

"That team out there has won one game but they're not playing like that," coach Lovie Smith said. "They're showing up every day, taking coaching, getting better and coming into the game and giving ourselves a chance to win."

Kansas City's streak of division titles is tied with the Rams (1973-79) for the second-longest in NFL history behind the Patriots, who captured 11 in a row in the AFC East from 2009-2019.

"I think one of the most difficult things in the National Football League is consistent success," Kansas City owner Clark Hunt said. "The rules are designed to make that difficult, whether that's the draft or the salary cap. So, it's a real testament to the job that general manager Brett Veach and coach Andy Reid have done over the last several years."

The Chiefs trailed for much of the day and were behind by five early in the fourth quarter when Mahomes dashed in from 5 yards out. His 2-point conversion pass to McKinnon came next to give Kansas City a 24-21 lead.

Mahomes thew for 336 yards and had touchdown passes of 20 and 4 yards.

Chiefs quarterback Patrick Mahomes crosses the goal line to score against the Texans.

Kansas City receiver Marquez Valdes-Scantling snags a bullet pass for a first half touchdown over Houston cornerback Tremon Smith.

Jerick McKinnon celebrates in the end zone after scoring the game-winning touchdown against the Texans.

MAHOMES #1 FAN!

Patrick Mahomes signs autographs for Chiefs fans in Houston after a thrilling win over the Texans in December, wrapping up the AFC West title in the process.

Chiefs 24, Seahawks 10   December 24, 2022

Keeping Pace

Chiefs Roll Past Seattle, Stay Tied with Bills for AFC's Best Record

KANSAS CITY, Mo. —

EVEN AS THE KANSAS CITY CHIEFS SQUEAKED OUT WINS THE PAST few weeks, coach Andy Reid lamented both the state of their inexperienced defense and their inability to put away struggling teams.

They showed massive improvement in both areas against Seattle on Saturday.

That youthful defense shut down Geno Smith and the slumping Seahawks offense, Patrick Mahomes threw two TD passes before running for a clinching score in the fourth quarter, and the Chiefs rolled to a 24-10 win that allowed them to keep pace with Buffalo for the best record in the AFC.

"I mentioned it the other way the last couple of weeks, that they need to get better," Reid said of his defense, which often has five or more rookies on the field at a time. "They're making progress and I thought they did a nice job today."

Indeed, the Chiefs stopped the Seahawks (7-8) twice on fourth down, picked off their Pro Bowl quarterback in the end zone and dealt coach Pete Carroll's team their fifth loss in six games along with a near-knockout blow to their playoff hopes.

Travis Kelce had six catches for 113 yards, and Kadarius Toney and Jerick McKinnon had touchdown catches, as the AFC West champion Chiefs (12-3) remain tied with the Bills — who hold the tiebreaker — with two games to go.

"We're on a mission here in Kansas City," Chiefs defensive end Frank Clark said, "and the goal is to finish the season strong. The last few weeks we haven't been getting the job done as far as finishing strong. A lot of tight games."

Kansas City has won 16 consecutive regular-season games against NFC opponents.

Kenneth Walker III was the biggest bright spot for Seattle, running for 107 yards but failing to reach the end zone. But the Chiefs mostly kept DK Metcalf in check, and Seattle didn't reach the end zone until the closing minutes of the game.

"We just couldn't get going and couldn't make first downs," Carroll said. "We got nothing going at all."

Much like the rest of the country, the cold weather that flooded the Midwest produced some frigid temperatures — the wind chill was minus-2 at kickoff, and that was an improvement over the previous two days. In fact, it had been so cold the tarp was frozen to the field when workers tried to remove it three hours before kickoff.

That didn't bother a half-dozen Seahawks, including DK Metcalf and his fellow wide receivers, who walked out of the tunnel bare-chested shortly afterward for their pregame warmups on the ice-covered field.

Maybe they weren't cold, but Seattle's offense was downright frigid.

Mahomes threw a pop pass to Toney to cap a 63-yard TD drive, then a pass to McKinnon out of the backfield a few minutes later for another score. And by the time Harrison Butker drilled a 47-yard field goal late in the half, the Chiefs had jumped out to a 17-0 lead.

Seattle got a field goal before halftime, much of the drive aided by defensive penalties.

Kansas City receiver Kadarius Toney celebrates after scoring a touchdown against the Seahawks.

Patrick Mahomes stretches the ball toward the pylon at the end of a touchdown run against Seattle.

Chiefs 27, Broncos 24   January 1, 2023

Going Through the Motions

Sluggish Chiefs Make it 15 Wins in a Row over Broncos

KANSAS CITY, Mo. —

PATRICK MAHOMES MOVED INTO THE RAREST OF COMPANY SUNDAY, JOINING
Tom Brady and Drew Brees as the only quarterbacks with multiple 5,000-yard passing seasons, and the Chiefs overcame another sloppy start to beat the Broncos for the 15th consecutive time and stay alive for the No. 1 seed in the AFC.

So everything must be good in Kansas City, right?

"There's not a lot satisfying for me," Mahomes said shortly after the 27-24 victory.

There was the pick he threw in the end zone and the mechanics that went awry in the second half. There was the fumbled punt return that led to a Denver touchdown, a sloppy snap on a point-after attempt and even a blocked field goal.

Yet the Chiefs (13-3) still managed to escape a 17-13 third-quarter deficit and rally for their fourth consecutive win.

"When I don't have my best stuff and guys step up and we still win football games," said Mahomes, who nevertheless finished with 328 yards passing and three touchdowns, "that's a good thing."

Jerick McKinnon had two touchdown catches while Blake Bell and Isiah Pacheco also scored for the Chiefs, who began the day tied with Buffalo for the best record in the AFC; the Bills play Cincinnati on Monday night.

"We'll watch it," Chiefs coach Andy Reid said with a smile.

For a while the Broncos (4-12) looked as if they might cap a chaotic week that began with the firing of first-year head coach Nathaniel Hackett in a stunning victory. But a late letdown by one of the league's best defenses, and another interception from embattled quarterback Russell Wilson, resulted in the first loss for interim coach Jerry Rosburg.

"I saw players and coaches digging in to do all they could possibly do to win that game," he said. "That all said, it wasn't good enough. It wasn't good enough and I'm heartbroken for those guys because they deserve a win."

Wilson threw for 222 yards and a touchdown while also running for a pair of scores, the second of them — after two costly penalties on the Kansas City defense — pulling Denver within 27-24 with 6:14 left in the game.

The Broncos got the ball back with just under four minutes to go, too, and picked up a quick first down. But the Kansas City defense stiffened near midfield, and Chris Jones sacked Wilson on fourth-and-2 to effectively end the game.

The Chiefs' sluggish start against the downtrodden Broncos wasn't all that surprising. They've habitually played down to the opposition, whether it was in their overtime win at Houston or their 34-28 victory over the Broncos three weeks ago.

But the Chiefs also have proven over the years their ability to strike quickly, and they did that after falling behind for the first time Sunday. Mahomes answered with long passes to Toney and McKinnon, a penalty on third down gave them a fresh set of downs, and McKinnon turned a screen pass into a touchdown reception for the fifth straight game.

Chiefs tight end Blake Bell celebrates scoring a touchdown against Denver on New Years Day.

Jerick McKinnon (1) and running back Isiah Pacheco run and smile to celebrate McKinnon's 3-yard touchdown reception in the fourth quarter.

Chiefs 31, Raiders 13 January 7, 2023

Peaking at Right Time

Mahomes Sets Record; Chiefs Earn Top Seed in AFC Playoffs

LAS VEGAS —

THE KANSAS CITY CHIEFS DON'T BELIEVE IN SIMPLY WRAPPING UP THE AFC'S top seed. They want to have fun doing it.

Late in the first half Saturday against the Las Vegas Raiders, the Chiefs huddled and spun in a circle, broke out into the shotgun with running back Jerick McKinnon taking a direct snap. He faked a handoff to Kadarius Toney and pitched to quarterback Patrick Mahomes, who then threw to Toney for a 9-yard touchdown.

But, it didn't count. A holding penalty brought back the play. The Chiefs then scored anyway to take full control of what became a 31-13 victory.

The play is called the Snow Globe or Arctic Circle, depending on who is asked. But, even if it didn't count, it underscored the Chiefs' creativity and willingness to have fun, even while playing for playoff positioning and a week off.

"We talked about it on the side, `Let's see if we can get some confusion going and throw something back.'" Mahomes said. "It worked. We just had the holding penalty. We got some good things going for the playoffs, and whatever we run has to work."

That, Chiefs coach Andy Reid said, was the bottom line.

"You do (want to make it fun), but you want to score, too," Reid said. "It's not fun when you're not doing that."

Almost lost was the NFL record for total yards in a season that Mahomes set. He passed for 202 yards and rushed for 29 against the Raiders, giving him 5,608 total yards this season. That surpassed the record of 5,562 yards set by Drew Brees in 2011 with the New Orleans Saints.

"Pat was on fire," Reid said. "He's throwing these (statistics) out there like they're nothing."

More than setting the mark, Mahomes helped ensure the top seed for the Chiefs (14-3) and a bye in the first round of the playoffs, which begin next weekend. Kansas City, however, is not assured of home-field advantage throughout the postseason.

Because Monday night's Buffalo-Cincinnati game was canceled, the Chiefs could wind up playing the Bills or Bengals in the AFC championship on a neutral field. The Buffalo-Cincinnati game initially was postponed after Bills safety Damar Hamlin went into cardiac arrest. Hamlin remains in critical condition, but is improving.

This was the first NFL game played since Hamlin was hospitalized. Both teams wore black shirts in warmups that read "LOVE FOR DAMAR" with his No. 3 in the middle. Mahomes also wore a hoodie that had a drawing of the player with "HAMLIN STRONG" below it.

Instead of a moment of silence before the game, the Allegiant Stadium public-address announcer asked fans to cheer on Hamlin's recovery.

"It was definitely weird," Mahomes said of returning to the field. "It's a game that you love, you play your entire life. It's brought so many great things to you. But, obviously, with the situation that happened Monday night with Damar, you still have that in the back of your mind. You want to be there for him, and there is so much stuff bigger than football."

Kansas City cornerback L'Jarius Sneed is all smiles after a 31-13 win over the Raiders to close out the regular season.

Chiefs defensive tackle Chris Jones sacks Las Vegas quarterback Jarrett Stidham.

Family Affair

Travis, Jason Kelce Stage A Family Reunion at Super Bowl

DONNA KELCE IS GOING TO HAVE TO PULL OUT THAT NOW-FAMILIAR CUSTOM jersey — the one with Kansas City Chiefs tight end Travis Kelce's front stitched to Philadelphia Eagles center Jason Kelce's back — one more time this season.

At least this time, she'll get to see her boys in person.

For the first time in Super Bowl history, a pair of siblings will play each other on the NFL's grandest stage. Kelce helped the Chiefs return to their third championship game in four seasons on Sunday night when they beat the Bengals for the AFC title, while Jason has the Eagles back for the second time in six years after their NFC title win over the 49ers.

"Cool scenario to be in, you know?" Travis Kelce said. "My mom can't lose."

Or maybe can't win.

Indeed, there have been plenty of famous NFL siblings over the years, and many had some memorable matchups: Peyton vs. Eli Manning, Tiki vs. Ronde Barber. But they never reached the same Super Bowl, or had to put their dear old mom in such a predicament, where one will be hoisting the Lombardi Trophy at the other one's expense.

"It's going to be an amazing feeling playing against him," added Travis, whose team has gotten the better of big brother's Eagles the last three matchups. "I respect everyone over there in the Eagles organization. You won't see me talk too much trash because of how much I love my brother. But it's going to be an emotional game, for sure."

Jason Kelce was even ever-so-briefly a Chiefs fan Sunday night, pulling on a Kansas City sweatshirt for about the three hours between the end of the Eagles' 31-7 rout of San Francisco and the finish of his little brother's 23-20 win over Cincinnati.

"That's it for the rest of the year," Jason said with a smile. "I am done being a Chiefs fan."

He'll leave that to mom and dad.

While her husband, Ed, has mostly kept private over the years, Donna has been a fixture as she crisscrosses the country to watch her boys. During wild-card weekend last year, she started in Tampa Bay watching the Eagles against the Buccaneers, then hopped a plane to Kansas City in time to watch the Chiefs play the Steelers at night.

She already has seen both of her sons win Super Bowls, too: The Eagles beat the Patriots in 2018 in Minneapolis, and the Chiefs rallied to beat the 49ers in Miami two years later.

She hasn't seen much of them lately, though. The way the playoff schedule worked out for the divisional round and the conference championship games it was impossible for Donna to make it to see both of her boys in person.

In any case, they've come a long way from their solidly middle-class upbringing in Cleveland Heights, Ohio.

Jason has been to six Pro Bowls and was just voted an All-Pro for the fifth time, and he's emerged as one of the best offensive linemen in Eagles history. Travis has been to eight Pro Bowls, just made a fourth All-Pro team and is second in NFL history to Jerry Rice in playoff catches, yards and touchdowns.

Travis Kelce, left, kisses his brother, Philadelphia Eagles center Jason Kelce, after a game in 2017.

Chiefs 27, Jaguars 20 January 21, 2023

Injury to Mahomes Mars Win

Hobbled Quarterback Leads Chiefs to Victory Over Jaguars

KANSAS CITY, Mo. —

PATRICK MAHOMES PLEADED WITH CHIEFS COACH ANDY REID TO LET HIM STAY in the game on Saturday.

He argued with trainers, assistant coaches and anyone else within earshot on the Kansas City sideline to let him play through an injured right ankle.

"I'm not coming out of a playoff game," Mahomes would say later, "unless they take me out."

Well, the Chiefs did, forcing him to get X-rays late in the first half of their divisional game against Jacksonville.

But when they came back negative, and Mahomes proved he could protect himself in the halftime locker room, Reid decided to let his All-Pro quarterback back on the field — and he gamely led them to victory.

Mahomes finished with 195 yards passing and two touchdowns, the second capping a 75-yard drive late in the fourth quarter, and lifted Kansas City to a 27-20 victory over the Jaguars and a spot in a fifth straight AFC championship game.

Mahomes also vowed to be ready for next week against the winner of Sunday's game between Cincinnati and Buffalo. If the Bengals win, they will be back at Arrowhead Stadium; if the Bills win, they're headed to Atlanta.

Chad Henne led a 98-yard touchdown drive while Mahomes was out. Travis Kelce had a career-high 14 catches for 98 yards and two scores. Marquez Valdes-Scantling hauled in the eventual clinching TD pass with about 7 minutes left in the game.

"It's a credit to the team I have around me, the coaches around me and the organization in general," Mahomes said. "We try to do whatever we can to be in this position, to get to the AFC championship game and find a way to the Super Bowl."

The Jaguars, who rallied from a 27-0 deficit to beat the Chargers in the wild-card round, squandered two chances to mount another late rally. The first ended when Jamal Agnew had the ball pop loose inside the Chiefs 5 with about 5 1/2 minutes to go, and the second when Jaylen Watson made a leaping, one-handed interception near midfield.

The Jaguars' last-gasp chance ended when Kansas City recovered an onside kick with 24 seconds to go.

Trevor Lawrence finished with 217 yards passing with a touchdown toss to Christian Kirk, who was briefly hurt midway through the fourth quarter but returned to finish the game. Travis Etienne added 62 yards rushing and a touchdown.

"When you get this far you don't want to only go this far," the Jaguars' Foyesade Oluokun said. "You want to keep going."

"I don't really have the words right now," Lawrence added. "The Chiefs did more today than we did."

Long before Mahomes hobbled to the sideline in pain, he was at his creative best, driving the Chiefs downfield on their opening possession.

There was a shortstop-style sidearm sling to JuJu Smith-Schuster, a key third down pass to Kelce as

Chiefs cornerback Jaylen Watson leaps to intercept a pass intended for Jaguars receiver Zay Jones during the AFC playoffs.

he was being dragged to the turf, and the flip pass to his tight end that gave Kansas City a 7-0 lead.

The Jaguars came right back, taking advantage of a big kickoff return and a short field.

Lawrence, whose four touchdown throws helped to stun the Chargers last week, proceeded to hit Kirk for the matching touchdown.

Then, the complexion of the game changed.

Mahomes was moving up in the pocket when Arden Key brought the full weight of his body down on the quarterback's ankle. Mahomes hobbled to the huddle and managed to get through three more plays to end the first quarter, then was on the field two more plays before Harrison Butker kicked a 50-yard field goal.

During the Jaguars' ensuing possession, Mahomes got into a heated argument with Reid and the training staff. He then threw down his coat and headed to the locker room, forcing Henne to take over midway through the second quarter, just as the 37-year-old journeyman did two years ago in a playoff win over Cleveland.

"Yeah, I did not want to go, and they kind of gave me the ultimatum that I wasn't going back in unless I went in there," said Mahomes, who cheered on Henne's 98-yard drive from the sideline, wearing a puffy winter coat on a cold, sleeting night.

As the second half began, though, that familiar red No. 15 jersey was trotting back onto the field.

"It was a short leash," Reid acknowledged. "If I felt like he wasn't

Kansas City defensive tackle Chris Jones rushes Jacksonville quarterback Trevor Lawrence.

able to handle it, he would have been out."

His right ankle heavily taped, Mahomes struggled to move around, but simply his presence seemed to calm the Chiefs — and their angst-filled fan base. Butker added a second 50-yard field goal late in the third quarter to extend the lead to 20-10, and when the AFC South champs answered with a touchdown of their own, so did the Chiefs.

Mahomes drove them downfield for one last score that proved to be the margin of victory.

"We know that if it's up to Pat, he's going to be in there. I'm sure he had some words with everyone on the sideline that he wanted to be in there as fast as possible," Kelce said afterward.

"It's just a different feeling when one-five is in there. He can make anything happen, even on one ankle."

Patrick Mahomes threw for two touchdowns despite an injured ankle against the Jaguars.

Chiefs receiver Marquez Valdes-Scantling makes a touchdown catch against Jacksonville.

Travis Kelce is tackled by Jaguars safety Rayshawn Jenkins after a catch.

Refined and Unstoppable

Chiefs Superstar Overhauled His Game, and Made Himself Even Better

THE EVOLUTION OF KANSAS CITY CHIEFS QUARTERBACK PATRICK MAHOMES has been a process to behold.

Mahomes has reinvented his game before our eyes, morphing — out of necessity — from a quick-strike superstar to one of the NFL's truly patient performers. And, most importantly, the Chiefs have remained among the league's elite teams while Mahomes, coach Andy Reid and offensive coordinator Eric Bieniemy developed a new formula.

The Chiefs' offense is much different from the one Mahomes took charge of during his record-setting second season in the NFL, and it's certainly less pleasing aesthetically for fans of long passes. But the object is to win games — and the Chiefs still look great in that area.

Mahomes has adjusted well to a new-look receiving corps that underwent a major offseason makeover. All-Pro wide receiver Tyreek Hill wanted more money than Chiefs management was willing to pay him, so Hill was traded to the Miami Dolphins.

It was fair to wonder how the Chiefs would fare without arguably the NFL's most dominant wideout. Some in the team's locker room likely had questions as well, because Hill is a game changer.

However, Mahomes, Reid and Bieniemy adjusted, leaning more on a running game buoyed by one of the league's best offensive lines, and using more short- to mid-range passes. That's also the area of the passing game in which All-Pro tight end Travis Kelce does his best work.

From the outside, the Chiefs' balanced offense looks beautiful, Hall of Famer Warren Moon said.

Moon, the only Black passer enshrined in the Pro Football Hall of Fame, said the Chiefs have played things perfectly.

"What I see from him [Mahomes] is a much more patient quarterback, and a lot of this comes from what he went through last year," Moon said. "[Opponents] tried to slow them down last year by playing a lot more 'umbrella' coverage.

"Teams wanted to see if he would keep taking the underneath routes, not get impatient and try to force it downfield. In the beginning last year, he was impatient. He did force it, because he was used to having all those big plays with Tyreek and the other guys.

"Now, this year, you can see he's being much more patient. He's taking his time to take his shots down the field. And what they're doing now is getting the ball out quickly. They're really giving guys a chance to run after the catch. It's not the big strikes down the field like they used to get in his first few years, but it's working."

The Chiefs' impressive running game is working quite well, too.

During the 2021 NFL draft, Kansas City general manager Brett Veach again proved that he's one of the league's most astute talent evaluators. Veach hit home runs in selecting center Creed Humphrey in the second round (63rd overall) out of the University of Oklahoma and guard Trey Smith in the sixth round (226th overall) from the University of Tennessee.

Quickly, Humphrey and Smith became key members of an O-line that helped the Chiefs establish a powerful run game. With Mahomes' passing ability, it's almost unfair that the Chiefs' offensive line is now so talented at run blocking, ESPN analyst Jeff Saturday said.

Patrick Mahomes points to the sky after the Chiefs beat the Bengals for the AFC Championship and a return to the Super Bowl.

Saturday, who played center for 14 years in the NFL and was a six-time Pro Bowler and a two-time All-Pro, said the Chiefs' offense oozes versatility.

"They have a very good offensive line. It's very physical. And you look at the way they're playing and using their run game, they're trusting that they can go do that [run the ball against anyone]," Saturday said. "That's allowing [Mahomes] to use all the pieces and parts of his offense.

Continuing along this path will only help Mahomes and the Chiefs, Moon said.

"This will make him more efficient for the remainder of his career," Moon said. "Especially as he gets older and when those legs won't let him run around as much and do all the things he does now.

"One day he's not going to be able to run around and do all of that stuff. But because he's learning to be more patient, reading the defense a little bit more and going to his second and third reads, these are the things that are going to make his career a lot longer."

And trust us on this: Mahomes doing things to elongate his career at a high level is the last thing Chiefs' opponents want.

Kansas City players gather around quarterback Patrick Mahomes before the start of the AFC Championship victory over Cincinnati.

Chiefs 23, Bengals 20 January 29, 2023

Super Again!

Mahomes Wills Chiefs Past Bengals, Allays Any Notion of Burrow Curse

KANSAS CITY, Mo. —

PATRICK MAHOMES WAS FORCED TO RELY ON HIS BADLY SPRAINED RIGHT ankle rather than his strong right arm when the Kansas City Chiefs were desperately driving with a chance to win the AFC championship.

The All-Pro quarterback, missing three wide receivers to injuries and battered himself, took off on a third-down play near midfield in another gut-check game with the Cincinnati Bengals. Mahomes strained to reach the mark he needed and was headed out of bounds when he felt the hands of Joseph Ossai send him sprawling into the bench.

The mad dash, coupled with the 15-yard penalty for a late hit, was all Kansas City needed.

Harrison Butker strode confidently onto the field, sent a 45-yard kick through cold, gusting wind over the crossbar with 3 seconds to go, and put the Chiefs back in the Super Bowl for the third time in four years with a 23-20 victory.

"I don't think we have any cigars," Mahomes said with a smile, "but we'll be ready to go in the Super Bowl."

It was vindication for the AFC West champions, who had lost three straight to their newfound nemeses, including a three-point overtime loss to Cincinnati in last year's conference title game. All of those defeats were by three points.

Now, the Chiefs are headed back to the big game.

Awaiting them is coach Andy Reid's old team, the Eagles, in the first matchup of Black quarterbacks in the Super Bowl with Mahomes and Philadelphia's Jalen Hurts. It will also feature a brother-against-brother showdown between Chiefs tight end Travis Kelce and Philadelphia center Jason Kelce.

"I've watched them all year," Mahomes said. "It's going to be a great challenge for us. But I'm going to celebrate this first."

Mahomes, who hurt his ankle against Jacksonville in the divisional round, threw for 326 yards and two touchdowns, even though he was missing three of his wide receivers to injuries by the end. Marquez Valdes-Scantling led with 116 yards and a touchdown, while Travis Kelce — bad back and all — had seven catches for 78 yards and a score.

"It's a tough bunch. My heart goes out to them, man, they're tough guys," Reid said. "They worked so hard this week. Pat and Kelce were both banged up a little bit. They pushed through and great things happened."

The Chiefs also managed to shut the mouths of the Bengals, some of whom had taken to calling their home "Burrowhead" for Joe Burrow, who had never lost to Kansas City. Even Cincinnati Mayor Aftab Pureval started in on the trash talk.

"I've got some wise words for that Cincinnati mayor," Kelce said. "Know your role and shut your mouth, you jabroni!"

Burrow, who was sacked five times and wobbly by the end, finished with 270 yards passing to go with a touchdown and two interceptions for the Bengals. Tee Higgins had six catches for 83 yards and the score.

This sequence shows the hit by the Bengals' Joseph Ossai on Patrick Mahomes on an out-of-bounds run late in the fourth quarter.

"We're not going to make it about one play. There was plenty of plays we left on the field today that could have put us in a better position," Bengals coach Zac Taylor said. "The character of this football team, that's never going to change. We've got the right people in the locker room, the right men leading this team and this organization.

"I know that this is a team that our city and our fan base can be proud of," Taylor added. "They represent themselves the right way, and we're going to fight, scratch and claw to be back in this position next year."

The Chiefs were able to do early what the Buffalo Bills could not in last week's divisional round: They ran roughshod over an ailing Bengals offensive line missing two starters to injury with another bothered by a sore knee.

Burrow was sacked three times in the first quarter alone and the Bengals offense did not gain a single yard.

Mahomes looked just fine on his sore ankle in leading Kansas City to a field goal on its opening possession. When the Chiefs got the ball back, Mahomes did it again, but only after Kadarius Toney failed to pull in a nifty throw for a would-be touchdown — the incompletion was upheld upon review.

Cincinnati finally got moving in the second quarter, but it also had to settle for Evan McPherson's chip-shot field goal.

So much for two of the league's highest-scoring offenses.

The Chiefs finally reached the end zone late in the second quarter when Mahomes hit Kelce, loosely covered by

Chiefs cornerback Jaylen Watson intercepts a pass intended for Cincinnati's Tee Higgins.

Jessie Bates III, with a fourth-down throw for the touchdown. The Bengals drove 90 yards in the closing minutes, but only added a field goal to get within 13-6 at the break.

Turns out their offense was just hitting its stride. And another classic was brewing.

After the Chiefs went three-and-out to start the second half, Burrow led the Bengals downfield, bolting through a yawning hole in the defense for a third-down conversion before hitting Higgins from 27 yards out to knot the game 13-all.

Mahomes, suddenly down three wide receivers to injuries and beginning to limp, gamely pressed on. He answered Burrow with a touchdown drive of his own, capped by a third-down throw to Valdes-Scantling to regain the lead.

The Chiefs had a chance to gain some breathing room later in the third quarter, but Mahomes somehow lost control of the ball before throwing a pass and the Bengals pounced on the fumble. Six players later — including an audacious fourth-down throw from Burrow to Ja'Marr Chase — Samaje Perine ran into the end zone to tie it at 20.

Burrow gave the Chiefs a chance when his deep throw to Higgins on third down was batted into the air and picked by rookie cornerback Josh Williams. Mahomes managed to move the Chiefs past midfield, but two runs went nowhere and his third-down throw to Jerick McKinnon was well short, forcing them to punt in Bengals territory.

Chiefs defensive end Mike Danna tackles Bengals quarterback Joe Burrow.

Kansas City's defense held, though, got a crucial sack from Chris Jones to force a punt with 39 seconds left, and shaky return man Skyy Moore broke free for 29 yards on the return. That gave Mahomes and the offense one more try.

"It was a tough road to get here. To win 10 in a row, it was a pretty incredible feat," Taylor said. "We came up short. We wanted to play longer than that, but really proud of these guys."

Kansas City kicker Harrison Butker connects on the game-winning field goal against Cincinnati.

Marquez Valdes-Scantling catches a touchdown in front of Cincinnati cornerback Mike Hilton before celebrating (left) in the end zone.

Bengals quarterback Joe Burrow and Chiefs quarterback Patrick Mahomes meet on the field after Kansas City won the AFC Championship in January.

Travis Kelce holds the Lamar Hunt Trophy alongside Patrick Mahomes after the Chiefs won the AFC Championship.